Release the Kingdom Within You

Identity - Equip - Release

I0170016

SALVATION

LESSON ONE

JOHN GOLD

Identity Teaching Series

ACKNOWLEDGEMENTS

I would like to thank Melodie Moss for her hours of work, wisdom, and guidance in bringing this book to fruition. You can see her wonderful and God-honoring work at

http://www.essenceoftheword.com

Dedication

This book is dedicated to the ones who will not settle, relent, give up and are ever seeking, knocking and striving to become all they can be in Christ and His Kingdom.

Table of Contents

PREFACE

M
Y CALL AND HEART for this series has one purpose, and that is to help others come into deep, dependent and true relationship with our Father, through Jesus Christ by the Holy Spirit. I fully believe today it is the will of God to establish His, not man's, church in the home and reestablish families, communities and beyond in taking back territory for His Kingdom.

Each of us is created, ordained and blessed to walk in an intimate relationship with our Creator and Father. This relationship has one purpose: That our Spirit and the Holy Spirit become one in Jesus to do the will of our Father in Heaven to impact this world.

For many decades, individuals have relied on the church for identity, equipping and growth. While the church has led many to Salvation, they failed to teach individuals their identity and equip them to become who they are created to be as Ambassadors of God's Kingdom. The Barna Group did a study and found that out of one hundred people who gained Salvation, more than 85% reverted back to their old lifestyle and thought processes within the first year of gaining Salvation. By not properly teaching identity and equipping new believers, we are now facing a mass exodus from the church due to lack of growth for the individual. You cannot effectively create disciples by listening to a Pastors sermon a couples a week.

I want to clarify identity and equipping. Identity refers to who God created you to be, your purpose and relationship with Him. The Holy Spirit gives giftings and talents such as the gift of healing, discernment and faith. Your identity and specific gifts or equipment gives you your purpose and the ability to properly live out that purpose. Think of a basketball player. They have a driving passion for basketball, they have natural talents for basketball, they excel at a certain position and are gifted enough to play the game. Practice, gaining wisdom and knowledge is the key to becoming a great basketball player, so it is with becoming who you are created to be in Christ.

I contend that anytime we become codependent on an institution or man for our relationship with Jesus, we will fail. I cannot become intimate and personal with you via another person or institution. My relationship with you has to be personal, and I have the responsibility on my own to further that relationship and make it stronger. If you have a rose bush and feed and nurture it, then you will produce amazing roses. If you neglect that rose bush, it will wither away and eventually die. It is our responsibility or lack thereof to either nurture or ignore our growth in the amazing relationship with Jesus Christ, His Word, and His Kingdom.

There is nothing wrong with attending church, but too many rely only on the church for their personal groth. Many become codependent on the local church and fail to learn how to develop their own personal relationship with Jesus. If the individual is not taught 'relationship' with Jesus to include how to study the Bible, how to worship, pray and awaken the Kingdom within them and release who they are created to be, the individual grows stagnant and eventually will give up out of frustration.

Remember falling in love? You would do anything to be with that person. Our desire is to get to know those we love, who we commit our lives to. Jesus gave us a way to know and learn through His Word.

There is nothing wrong with gaining wisdom from man or church, but the responsibility at the end of the day for our relationship with Jesus is ours alone. For instance, you will read this teaching and hopefully gain wisdom and understanding to further your relationship with Jesus. You're not reading this to gain a relationship with me. This booklet is just a simple tool to help you grow closer to Jesus, a little water for your rose bush so to speak. So, let us explore together and journey to grow in the intimacy of Jesus beginning with Salvation.

INTRODUCTION

T HE BEST PLACE TO START ON OUR journey of releasing the Kingdom within you is at the very beginning... Salvation. As part of the Identity Teaching Series, we will explore the depths and what it truly means to receive Salvation in its fullness. Come with me now as we explore the wonder and love of Salvation.

You Are Loved

You are god's chosen. god chose you even if you don't want to accept it. He chose you because He loves you with an everlasting love. Before God created the foundations of the Earth, He chose you, for He knew you before your mother and father ever crossed paths. You are not a mistake, accident, blunder or miscalculation. You are chosen, loved and watched over. God is your protector whom neither sleeps nor slumbers. You are loved.

The hairs on your head are numbered. Not counted, but numbered. Even if they were counted, that would show His love and attention for you, but to be individually numbered means that if one of your hairs were to fall out, God would be able to tell you that it was hair number three thousand seven hundred and twenty-two. You are loved. You are loved. I can't say it enough; never forget that. Your fingerprints are vastly different to anyone else's fingerprints on earth. God never repeated your fingertips on anyone else.

You are uniquely created, you are fearfully and wonderfully made distinctly different from anybody else, past, present or future. No one has ever walked on this Earth with the same gifts, talents and anointing on their life as you. You are loved even in your mistakes. God loves you even in your bad decisions. God loves you. You are so loved, no weapon formed against you shall prosper. You are protected, and not just protected, but divinely protected. Nothing can touch you. Look around the room you are in now. You may not be able to see what's around you, but believe me when I tell you that there are angels around you to protect you, to guide you, to lead you and to comfort you.

From the moment you were born, God assigned angels to protect you. Psalms 91, verse 11: for He will give His angels charge concerning you to guard you in all your ways. Luke 4 verse 10: for it is written He will command His angels concerning you, to guard you carefully. You are precious to God, and He loves you.

This is what He's saying to you at this moment: I love you so much! I chose you, not Billy, not John, not Barbara; I chose you! I love you more than you could ever know or understand. Even in the days you walked as a child to an adult, so many things I have kept from harming you. I have kept you, and you didn't even know it. I have guarded you in moments, and you didn't even know it. I have stopped so many things in your life that you did not have any idea what was about to happen, but you'd never know it. I was there with you, even in the darkest hours of your life. I was there when the nights were long. I was there because I am the same God yesterday, today and forever.

I AM, I keep My word, and I say I will never leave you, neither will I forsake you. Have faith that you are My child. You are precious to Me.

-GOD

At this time, I would like for you (saved or not) to go to a quiet place and, with all your heart, ask Jesus to allow you to experience His love. I promise within a short time you will have an encounter with the full love of Jesus.

CHAPTER ONE

The Roots of Sin

"Whoever commits sin also commits lawlessness, and sin is lawlessness. And you know that He was manifested to take away our sins, and in Him there is no sin. Whoever abides in Him does not sin. Whoever sins has neither seen Him nor known Him"

—Apostle John

WE NEED AN UNDERSTANDING of sin so that we can understand Salvation. Some may ask the legitimate question: Why should I be saved? It is a good question, so let us explore the who, what, why and how to shed light on the question of Salvation. Let us start our exploration from the beginning by asking: What is sin?

The origin of sin first came with the rebellion of the cherub angel Lucifer in Heaven. (Ezekiel 28:13-16) Lucifer was cast out of Eden upon God's Holy Mountain (Mount Zion in Jerusalem.) Lucifer then re-entered the garden to entice and twist the word of God by tempting Eve. Adam, instead of stopping Eve, joined with her and, by choice, sinned, and their transgression infected the rest of humanity until the finished work of Christ on the Cross. Be it an outright rebellion against God, an iniquity or a fault, they are all choices made by us all.

How did evil manifest itself in a perfect creature? It may be good to mention that evil is not a created thing; it is not a creature and has no independent being. Also, evil has no standard as goodness does; it is a lack, a deficiency, a falling short of the standard of God's perfect goodness. All sin, no matter how trivial it may seem, falls short of moral perfection. God is always consistent with His perfect nature (Deuteronomy 32:4.) All sin, therefore, must come from Lucifer, and the desire for evil comes from within Lucifer. 14 But each one is tempted when he is drawn away by his own desires and enticed. 15 Then, when desire has conceived, it gives birth to sin; and sin, when it is full-grown, brings forth death -James 1:14-15. Sin was found in Lucifer due to a choice that the cherub angel made to seek something other than what God had chosen for him. Any time we seek something other than God's choice, we sin.

To say sin originated within God's creation does not mean God was surprised or caught unaware by it. Although God did not bring about sin, He certainly allowed it or it would not exist, since God is sovereign over all things. It's true that He could have prevented sin, but that would have meant stripping His creation of its free will (Daniel 4:17; Psalm 33:10-11.) All His ways are good. In Him is *"no darkness at all"* (1 John 1:5), and He is right now working all things for His good pleasure (Romans 8:28; Isaiah 46:9-10.)

The mystery of evil and why God has allowed its reality with all the suffering it causes may never be fully known in this world, but scripture assures that evil is temporary. Once the culmination of God's redemptive plan is complete, Jesus Christ will have destroyed the devil's work forever (1 John 3:8.)

Let us discover what the word 'sin' means. In Hebrew, the original language of the word of God, 'sin' has three meanings.

The word 'Pesha,' or 'Trespass,' describes a sin done out of rebelliousness. The word 'Aveira' means transgression, or to cross over a boundary. And the word 'Avone,' or 'Iniquity,' means a sin done out of moral failing.

- **Pesha** (Trespass) - An intentional and deliberate sin; an action committed in deliberate defiance of God.
- **Aveira** (Transgression) – To pass or cross over a moral boundary, to do a bad deed to another.
- **Avon** (Iniquity) – This is a sin of lust or uncontrollable emotion. It is a sin done knowingly in selfishness and not done to defy God. The root meaning is perversity, moral evil.

CHAPTER TWO

The Roots of Salvation

"How shall we escape if we neglect so great a salvation?"

—Apostle Paul

THE HEBREW ROOT WORD FOR SALVATION is 'Yesha' (the root form of the name 'Jesus' or, in Hebrew, 'Yeshua') Yesha means freedom from what binds or restricts and consequently effects deliverance.

History of Salvation

Genesis 3: In the Garden of Eden, when Eve and then Adam ate the fruit from the tree of good and evil, sin was released upon the earth. Adam and Eve knew nothing of guilt, shame or fear as they walked with God daily. Imagine that, walking with Jesus every day in paradise. God had ordered them not to eat of the tree of good and evil; Eve was tempted by the words of the devil and made the choice to eat, then Eve talked Adam into sharing the fruit with her, and then Adam made a choice, and he ate. In a moment, by their choice of disobedience, Adam and Eve defied God, and so sin entered the world.

Immediately, Adam and Eve's eyes were opened; guilt, shame and fear came upon them, and they attempted to cover their nakedness. Then they heard the sound of the Lord walking in the garden and hid themselves. The Lord called out to them and questioned them concerning what they had done. Had Adam and Eve admitted what they had done, maybe things would have turned out differently, but they did not take responsibility for their actions and, rather, placed blame.

Adam blamed Eve and Eve blamed the serpent. Because of this, God had to judge them, and he did. Eve received her judgment that her sorrow would multiply, childbirth would be painful, she will desire her husband and he will rule over her.

God cursed the ground; Adam and his descendants would have to toil and eat what the ground produced by the sweat of their brow. God then created death for man, telling Adam, "from the dust you were created, and to the dust you will return. The wages of sin are death." But God already had a plan.

God made them tunics of skin and clothed them. Wait! God did what? God, at this time, took a sheep and placed it before Adam and Eve. God then slaughtered the sheep, deskinned the animal and clothed Adam and Eve. Imagine this. Adam and Eve witnessed this innocent sheep get slaughtered because of what they did, and with this sheep's skin they were covered. This was a foretelling of Jesus' slaughter and how, by His crucifixion, His blood sacrifice covers us.

Genesis 22: God tested His most faithful servant Abraham by requesting that Abraham take his son Isaac to Mount Moriah (Mount Moriah today is Jerusalem, more specifically the Temple Mount.) Abraham built an altar, on top of the alter he set the wood for the fire and on top bound his son and placed his son Isaac.

With the knife, Abraham drew back with an outstretched hand to sacrifice his son, and the Angel of the Lord stopped him.

Let's stop here a moment.

Abraham waited twenty-five years for his son Isaac to be born, and now God wanted him to sacrifice him? At this time, it is believed Isaac was in his mid-twenties.

Abraham and his family knew they were sinners, and often built an altar and sacrificed a lamb to atone for their sins. As in the Garden of Eden, we know the price for sin is death. Isaac had observed this sin sacrifice and participated with his father numerous times. In verse 5 of Genesis 22, Abraham says something odd.

And Abraham said to his young men, "Stay here with the donkey; the lad and I will go yonder and worship, and we will come back to you."

Abraham knew the sacrifice of sin was death, so why did Abraham say that the lad and I will come back to you? Did Abraham have such faith in God that he trusted God had a plan to raise Isaac from the dead after the sacrifice? Hebrews 11:17-19 gives us insight into what Abraham was thinking this day.

17 By faith Abraham, when he was tested, offered up Isaac, and he who had received the promises offered up his only begotten son, 18of whom it was said, *"In Isaac your seed shall be called,"* 19 concluding that God was able to raise him up, even from the dead, from which he also received him in a figurative sense.

In faith, Abraham trusted God would indeed raise Isaac from the dead.

Another interesting thing Abraham said. Isaac knew there were rocks to build the altar, he carried the wood for the fire, but Isaac asks his father on the way to Moriah, "where is the lamb for the burnt offering?" Abraham responds in verse 8: *"My son, God will provide for Himself the lamb for a burnt offering."* Ponder this for a few moments.

Let's return.

11 But the Angel of the LORD called to him from heaven and said, "Abraham, Abraham!"

So he said, *"Here I am."*

12 And He said, *"Do not lay your hand on the lad, or do anything to him; for now I know that you fear God since you have not withheld your son, your only son, from Me."*

13 Then Abraham lifted his eyes and looked, and there behind him was a ram caught in a thicket by its horns. So Abraham went and took the ram, and offered it up for a burnt offering instead of his son. 14 And Abraham called the name of the place, [c]The-LORD-Will-Provide; as it is said to this day, *"In the Mount of the LORD it shall be provided."*

15 Then the Angel of the LORD called to Abraham a second time out of heaven, 16 and said: *"By Myself I have sworn, says the LORD, because you have done this thing, and have not withheld your son, your only son— 17 blessing I will bless you, and multiplying I will multiply your descendants as the stars of the Heaven and as the sand which is on the seashore; and your descendants shall possess the gate of their enemies. 18 In your seed, all the nations of the earth shall be blessed because you have obeyed My voice."* 19 So Abraham returned to his young men, and they rose and went together to Beersheba; and Abraham dwelt at Beersheba.

Notice in verse 13 it says there was a ram caught in the thicket by his horns. Does this remind us of the crown of thorns Jesus wore?

God has shown us His plan of Salvation through Adam and Eve, and now through Abraham and Isaac. Now let us understand Salvation through the Bible vertically and horizontally.

Two Perspectives

We will seek to understand God's global plan of Salvation from two perspectives: horizontally and vertically. We will first consider the Bible horizontally, as an unfolding narrative down through history. This will involve viewing God's plan of Salvation regarding creation, the fall, redemption, and consummation. Then we will consider God's plan of salvation vertically, looking down on the Bible from above. This will be done by centering upon God, man, Christ, repentance, and faith, in that order.

Understanding God's Plan of Salvation Horizontally

Creation

God made the world and all that is in it (Gen. 1:1.) He created Adam and Eve, the first man and the first woman, in his image (Gen. 1:26–28,) giving them the task of populating the world and subduing it (Gen. 1:28.) All of God's creation was *"very good"* (Gen. 1:31.) The world is neither a haphazard collection of atoms nor is it inherently bad. God created the world, and it was good.

Fall

Adam and Eve rejected God's good rule, determining to be their own lords (Gen. 3:1–7.) This rebellion plunged all of humanity into sin, darkness, misery, and death, for Adam represented, and thus involved, the entire human race in his actions (Rom. 5:12; 1 Cor. 15:21–22.) Since the fall, human history has been ravaged with the carnage of sickness, selfishness, strife, and other manifestations of Adam's horrific rebellion, and we are unable, in ourselves, to set things right.

Redemption

Even in Eden, God began to promise that sin and Satan would not get the last word (Gen. 3:15.) And indeed, in the fullness of time, God sent his own Son to deliver his people from bondage to sin and death (Gal. 4:4–5.) Through the Son's atoning death on the cross and resurrection from the grave, redemption was accomplished, and the decisive fulfillment of all the Old Testament promises has been launched (Mark 1:14–15; 2 Cor. 1:20.) Through the work of the Holy Spirit, opening the eyes of the spiritually blind and bringing life, redemption is applied (Rom. 8:1–11; 1 Cor. 2:10–16.)

Consummation

One day God's Son will come to Earth again, this time openly and without any question as to who he is (Phil 2:10–11; Rev. 19:11–16.) He will come in final judgment and restore the Earth to what it was always meant to be, only this time without any threat of Satan, sin, and death (Rev. 21:1–22:5.) What God intended, according to the first two chapters of the Bible, appears as his final and glorious achievement in the last two chapters of the Bible. Christ will establish what the Bible calls the new Heavens and the new Earth (e.g., Isa. 65:17,) where the original goodness and perfection of Eden will be restored, and humanity will flourish in a renewed creation that has been set free from its bondage to decay (Rom. 8:21.)

Understanding God's Plan of Salvation Vertically

<u>God</u>

God created human beings to bring him glory (Isa. 43:6–7; 1 Cor. 10:31.) Anyone who seeks his own glory, as Adam did, sins against God and is subject to God's judgment (Acts 12:20–23.) All things happen according to God's plan and serve to glorify him (Eph. 1:11–12.) Every culture has a view of its god or gods that affects how people conduct their lives, but the Bible says that there is only one true God (Deut. 6:4; Jer. 14:22.) It is idolatry to worship any other god (Ex. 20:3–6.) God is the absolute transcendent governor of the universe.

God is also holy, meaning that he is utterly pure and incapable of sin or evil (Isa. 6:1–5.) He likewise calls his people to be holy (1 Pet. 1:15–16.) God is just, meaning that he is unswerving in doing what is morally right. The Bible expresses this absolute moral purity and righteousness by saying that "*God is light*" (1 John 1:5.)

The Bible also teaches that "*God is love*"—loving kindness is the very heart of who God is (Ex. 34:6–7; Matt. 11:29.) He is "*the God of all grace*" (1 Pet. 5:10.) God is not only supremely other in purity, but also supremely merciful in impulse.

Recognizing who God is, we realize that there is a massive problem facing humanity. We can understand the nature of this problem by looking at who man is in relation to who God is.

Man

Having been created in God's image and yet having chosen to break free from trusting submission to him, Adam rebelled, and through him sin entered the world (Rom. 5:12–14.) All human beings continue to bear the image of God in some sense (Gen. 9:5–6,) though we are now marred by sin. As God-resisting sinners, we are born with an inherent, spiritual blindness and hostility to God (Rom. 3:9–19.) We are his settled enemies.

We need, therefore, to be reconciled to him. We require a mediator to bridge the humanly unbridgeable gap between our sinfulness and God's holiness (1 Tim. 2:5–6.) We are unable to glorify God as he created us to do (Rom. 3:23.) God is rightly angry with us, and we cannot save ourselves from his wrath—that is, his judicial retribution (John 3:18; Eph. 2:1–3.) If we are to be saved at all, it will have to be by the work of someone else, someone who is qualified to save us. Sacrificing to spirits, appeasing ancestors, and cultural rituals to ward off evil spirits cannot save us from the coming wrath.

Jesus Christ

In his great mercy, God sent his Son to bear the wrath that must fall on human sin (John 3:16; 1 John 4:10.) How is it that Jesus saves us from the wrath of God? Here we consider who Jesus is (his person) and what he did (his work.)

Jesus is fully God, equal with the Father. To see Him is to see God the Father (John 10:30). It is necessary that Jesus if he is to save us, be fully divine because the payment for sin is one that mere mortals cannot pay—for their sin is against an infinitely beautiful and glorious God, and so they are infinitely guilty. As God, however,

Jesus is qualified to pay the penalty for sins committed against God. Yet Jesus is also fully man (Gal. 4:4.) He became like us in every way, yet without sinning (Heb. 2:16–18.) Jesus is therefore uniquely fitted to pay the penalty we owe. This is who Jesus is.

What did Jesus do? As the second Adam, he succeeded where Adam failed (Rom. 5:12–19.) This is supremely seen in Jesus' death and resurrection. On the cross, Jesus took our place, suffering and dying for us, so that we might be restored to our Creator (Isa. 53:4–6; 1 Pet. 2:24; 3:18; 1 Cor. 15:3–4.) God poured out all of his holy wrath on his beloved Son and judged him in our place so that we can be set free (2 Cor. 5:21; Gal. 3:13.) United with him not only in his death but also in his resurrection, we are given new life (Rom. 6:4; 1 Pet. 1:3.) Jesus' bodily resurrection means that the final resurrection has, in him, already begun (1 Cor. 15:20–22.) Jesus' earthly life, too, is relevant to our Salvation. Jesus obeyed God perfectly in our place (Heb. 4:15) so that God sees his obedience as our own. Because of Jesus' perfect righteousness, those who are in Christ stand righteous before God (1 Cor. 1:30; 2 Cor. 5:21.)

Jesus is the Savior we need to rescue us from God's wrath. How then does his saving work become a reality for any one of us?

Repentance and Faith

The proper response to the work of Christ on our behalf is repentance and faith (Mark 1:15; Acts 2:37–38; 20:21.) These twin-heart responses together form the healthy, biblical, Spirit-led activity of those who have understood God, their sin, and Jesus as Savior.

Repentance is a turning from sin and idolatry to serve the true and living God (Ezek. 14:6; 1 Thess. 1:9). This does not mean that believers will not struggle with sin anymore but rather that sin no longer has dominion over us (Rom. 6:12.) Sin no longer sits on the throne of the believer's heart.

If repentance is a turning from, faith is a turning to—from sin to Christ. Faith is trusting Christ as our Savior and confessing him as Lord (Rom. 10:9–10.) It is believing that God exists and is near to those who seek him wholeheartedly (Heb. 11:6.) Faith is our glad receiving and resting in the work of Christ. It means that we cast ourselves on Christ alone for the forgiveness of our sins and the fulfillment of all God's promises for us in Christ (Titus 3:4–7.) Everyone must exercise faith in Christ to be saved. Even faith, however, is a gift from God (Eph. 2:8–9; Phil. 1:29.) True faith results in a life of loving obedience (Eph. 2:8–10; James 2:14–26) as the Holy Spirit produces Christlike fruit in the believer (Gal. 5:22–25.) This obedience never earns God's approval, for Christ has already earned God's approval for us. At the same time, the Bible is clear that while obedience does not win our Salvation, the absence of grateful obedience indicates the absence of Salvation (Eph. 5:1–2; Col. 3:1.)

In the end, God himself is supremely glorified in his great plan of Salvation. One day every knee will bow, and every tongue will confess Jesus as Lord to the glory of God the Father (Phil. 2:10–11.) When the plan of God is complete, we will surely see God as he is and will be like him (1 John 3:2.) We will join with millions of believers from all over the world, "from every tribe and language and people and nation" (Rev. 5:9,) who have put their faith in Christ for Salvation. We will all worship God forever, with the angels saying "*Amen*" to our worship (Rev. 7:9–12.) On that day, the glory of the Lord will fill the earth as the waters fill the sea (Hab. 2:14.)

CHAPTER THREE

In the Garden

The Bible is the story of two gardens. Eden and Gethsemane. In the first, Adam took a fall. In the second, Jesus took a stand.

—Max Lucado

WHILE THE RICH HISTORY OF THE "*Last Supper*," or Passover Seder, is fascinating, I will begin this chapter in the olive groves near the Gethsemane on the Mount of Olives. Let me clarify.

At the time of Jesus, at the foot of the Mount of Olives, the season for olive pressing had ended. A Gethsemane, or Gat Shmanim in Hebrew, means olive-press. A Gethsemane is a half above and half below ground structure which was used to press and process the oil from olives. At the time of Passover in Jerusalem, it was crowded. Jesus and His disciples temporarily lived in the Gethsemane, which was naturally adjacent to the grove of olive trees. There is another reason as well. It was custom after the Passover meal, or Seder, to spend the night in solitude, prayer and rest. It is also the Night of Watching—Leil Shimurim in Hebrew—from Exodus 12:42. This is a time frame about midnight to remember the deliverance out of Egypt, but also looking or watching for the redemption by Messiah as well.

36 Then Jesus came with them to a place called Gethsemane, and said to the disciples, *"Sit here while I go and pray over there."* 37 And He took with Him Peter and the two sons of Zebedee, and He began to be sorrowful and deeply distressed. 38 Then He said to them, *"My soul is exceedingly sorrowful, even to death. Stay here and watch with me."*(Matthew 26:36-46)

It was not like Jesus to become sorrowful and deeply distressed, especially after the joyful time of the Passover meal, but why was He? Beloved, we often think only of Christ's suffering on the Cross. I contend Jesus' suffering began in the grove of olive trees on the Mount of Olives.

41 And He was withdrawn from them about a stone's throw, and He knelt down and prayed, 42 saying, *"Father, if it is Your will, take this cup away from Me; nevertheless not My will, but Yours, be done."* 43 [f]Then an angel appeared to Him from heaven, strengthening Him. 44 And being in agony, He prayed more earnestly. Then His sweat became like great drops of blood falling down to the ground. Luke 22:41-43

Why does Jesus mention a *"cup?"* If you study the Passover Seder, there are four cups and one cup set aside. This fifth cup is the cup of God's wrath. Jesus had to drink the cup of God's wrath for us. Beloved, I cannot even conceive of taking on God's wrath for all humanity, can you? This would truly explain why Jesus was in such great distress, to the point He was sweating His blood. The medical term for sweating blood, or blood sweat, is hematohidrosis; a condition in which capillary blood vessels that feed the sweat glands rupture, causing them to exude blood. Blood sweat occurs under conditions of acute fear and severe physical or emotional stress. Let this sink in for a bit, meditate on this for a few moments as we consider the suffering of our Salvation.

40 Then He came to the disciples and found them sleeping, and said to Peter, *"What! Could you not watch with Me one hour? 41 Watch and pray, lest you enter into temptation. The spirit indeed is willing, but the flesh is weak."* (Matthew 26:41)

This scripture takes us back to the 'Night of Watching' and now may make a little more sense. Peter, James, and John fell asleep during a crucial time when they were supposed to be night watching, and not only that, but they saw Jesus was in great distress but slept anyways. We are all guilty of sleeping when we should be watching and praying. Can you recall times when you should have prayed but instead chose to sleep instead? This reminds me of the scripture in Matthew 5 41 And whoever compels you to go one mile, go with him two. 42 Give to him who asks you, and from him who wants to borrow from you do not turn away. How many times have you been asked to pray for a brother or sister, said you would, but then did not?

Beloved, the spiritual impact of this night is immense. Jesus, in partaking of the cup of God's wrath, is drinking the judgment of God for all humanity's wicked ways. Jesus drank the horrid judgment of God. Earlier, we addressed the three types of sin:

The word Pesha, or 'Trespass,' means a sin done out of rebelliousness. The word Aveira means 'Transgression,' to cross over a boundary. And the word Avone, or 'Iniquity,' means a sin done out of moral failing.

I find it amazing that the three types of sin coincide with the three types of punishment Jesus took upon Himself.

Cup of God's Wrath – Jesus taking on the punishment or judgment of God for humanity upon Himself.

The flogging of Jesus' body – Jesus taking our infirmities or sickness and disease upon Himself.

The crucifixion on Golgotha – Jesus taking on all past, present and future sin of humanity unto Himself on our behalf.

Too often we take what Christ did for us for granted. The next time you take communion or the remembrance of what Jesus did for us, may we stop and ponder fully what was done by Christ. May we never neglect such a great Salvation.

CHAPTER FOUR

By His Stripes

"Peter must have thought, "Who am I compared to Mr. Faithfulness (John)?"
But Jesus clarified the issue. John was responsible for John. Peter was
responsible for Peter. And each had only one command to heed: "Follow Me."

—Charles R. Swindoll

N OW I WANT TO PROCEED TO later that day after Jesus' arrest when Pontius Pilate ordered the flogging from where we get the prophetic scripture of Isaiah 53:5 But He was wounded for our transgressions, He was bruised for our iniquities; The chastisement for our peace was upon Him, And by his stripes we are healed.

In Dr. William D. Edwards' book On the Physical Death of Jesus Christ, Dr. Edwards explains Roman flogging. "Flogging was a legal preliminary to every Roman execution, and only women and Roman senators or soldiers (except in cases of desertion) were exempt. The usual instrument was a short whip with several single or braided leather thongs of variable lengths, in which small iron balls or sharp pieces of sheep bones were tied at intervals. For scourging, the man was stripped of his clothing, and his hands were tied to an upright post. The back, buttocks, and legs were flogged either by two soldiers (lictors) or by one who alternated positions. The severity of the scourging depended on the disposition of the lictors and was intended to weaken the victim to a state just short of collapse or death. As the Roman soldiers repeatedly struck the victim's back with full force, the iron balls would cause deep contusions, and the leather thongs and sheep bones would cut into the skin and subcutaneous tissues. Then, as the flogging continued, the lacerations would tear into the underlying skeletal muscles and produce quivering ribbons of bleeding flesh. Pain and blood loss generally set the stage for circulatory shock. The extent of blood loss may well have determined how long the victim would survive on the cross. After the scourging, the soldiers often taunted their victim."

The greatest depiction of this horrific event as our savior was beaten within an inch of His life is Mel Gibson's film The Passion of the Christ, where we truly observe Jesus torturous suffering and mocking.

Isaiah 53:5 states…

5 But He was wounded for our transgressions,

He was bruised for our iniquities;

The chastisement for our peace was upon Him,

And by His stripes we are healed.

If you are not sure what the words transgressions, iniquities or chastisement means, then this is your opportunity to grow. If you truly want to grow, look these words up and obtain the definitions in Hebrew.

As Christ was being flogged, with each contact made upon His body, we could say, *"there goes cancer, there goes diabetes, there goes this or that ailment, sickness or disease."* The purpose or benefit for everything Jesus did was for us and not Himself.

I have friends whose faith, like concrete, is so great they simply never get sick. They believe so strongly, reject anyone telling them any different, and live by Isaiah 53:5. They do not have fear, doubt or unbelief. They get ridiculed by others out of jealousy, but the fact remains they simply do not get sick. We need to build up our faith and believing so we may enjoy a life of freedom from what ails us.

26 But Jesus looked at them and said to them, *"With men this is impossible, but with God all things are possible."* Matthew 19:26

CHAPTER FIVE

It is finished

"Sooner or later I will realize that the very things I most desperately need are the very things I am unable to give myself. Therefore, I will either be left despising the fact that I am doomed to live out a life that is perpetually empty, or I will realize that an empty tomb is the single thing that will eternally fill me."

— Craig D. Lounsbrough

N DR. C. TRUMAN DAVIS BOOK The Passion of the Christ from a Medical View, we can get a glimpse from a physical standpoint of Jesus' crucifixion.

<u>The Physical Torment</u>

The crucifixion begins. Jesus is quickly thrown backward with His shoulders against the wood. (Crucifixes today show the nails through the palms. Roman historical accounts have shown the nails are driven between the small bones of the wrists and not through the palms. Nails driven through the palms will strip out between the fingers when they support the weight of a human body. The misconception may have come about through a misunderstanding of Jesus' words to Thomas, "*Observe my hands.*" Anatomists, both modern and ancient, have always considered the wrists as part of the hand.)

The legionnaire drives a heavy, square wrought-iron nail through the wrist and deep into the wood. The left foot is pressed backward against the right foot, and a nail is driven through the arch of each, leaving the knees moderately flexed. The Victim is now crucified. As He slowly sags down with more weight on the nails in the wrists, excruciating, fiery pain shoots along the fingers and up the arms - the nails in the wrists are putting pressure on the median nerves. As He pushes Himself upward to avoid this stretching torment, He places His full weight on the nail through His feet. Again, there is the searing agony of the nail tearing through the nerves between the metatarsal bones of the feet.

As the arms fatigue, waves of cramps knot them in deep, relentless pain. With these cramps comes the inability to push Himself upward. Hanging by His arms, the pectoral muscles are paralyzed, and the intercostal muscles are unable to act. Air can be drawn into the lungs, but cannot be exhaled. Finally, carbon dioxide builds up in the lungs and the bloodstream, and the cramps partially subside. Spasmodically, He can push Himself upward to exhale and bring in the life-giving oxygen.

Hours of this pain, cycles of twisting, joint-rendering cramps, intermittent partial asphyxiation, searing pain as tissue is torn from His lacerated back as He moves up and down against the rough timber. Then another agony begins; a crushing pain deep in the chest as the pericardium slowly fills with serum and begins to compress the heart. It is now almost over; the loss of tissue fluids has reached a critical level. The compressed heart is struggling to pump. The tortured lungs are making a frantic effort to gasp in small gulps of air.

A sponge soaked in the cheap, sour wine is lifted to His lips. He apparently doesn't take any of the liquid. The body of Jesus is now in extremis, and He can feel the chill of death creeping through His tissues. This realization brings out His words ..."*It is finished!*"

His mission of atonement has been completed. Finally, He can allow His body to die. With one last surge of strength, He once again presses His torn feet against the nail, straightens His legs, takes a deeper breath, and utters His last cry, "*Father, into Thy hands, I commit My Spirit.*"

The Psychological Torment

At the time of the crucifixion, the Jews were a much more modest society than we are today, and while we see pictures of Jesus on the cross covered with a loincloth, this is simply untrue. Jesus was humiliated by being naked upon the cross, being stripped of everything in a public place. There stood not only the Roman soldiers but members of the Sanhedrin, his friends and finally his mother. In his nakedness, through medical evidence, Jesus would have urinated and defecated due to the combined torture of flogging and crucifixion. Jesus was openly mocked, and many of his disciples abandoned him. Beloved, we get embarrassed and humiliated in small matters, but take a moment and put yourself on that cross, enduring the most humiliating experience of your life. Ponder this a moment.

The Spiritual Torment

The psychological and physical torment for us is inconceivable. And yet, the worst torment that Jesus faced was spiritual. It was the first time, even before creation, that Jesus was separated and forsaken by His Father while being judged for the sins of humanity. The author of Hebrews writes, "*it is a terrifying thing to fall into the hands of the living God*" (Hebrews 10:31,) and Jesus, by his own choice, took this terror for us over a three to six-hour period that final day on Golgotha.

Beloved, I am reminded of Hebrews 2:3-4, 3 how shall we escape if we neglect so great a salvation, which at the first began to be spoken by the Lord, and was confirmed to us by those who heard Him, 4 God also bearing witness both with signs and wonders, with various miracles, and gifts[a] of the Holy Spirit, according to His own will?

As I saw the depiction of Christ being flogged in Mel Gibson's film The Passion of the Christ, I wanted to jump out of my seat in the movie theater and scream at the top of my lungs, "*STOP!*" I almost did, because I could not bear anyone taking a beating like that, much less Jesus. As the movie came to the crucifixion scene, I had righteous anger come over me towards myself, and I thought, '*how dare I!? How dare I live the lazy and unfruitful life I had been living as a so-called Christian, not taking seriously such a great Salvation?* By the time I walked out of that theater many years ago, I had begun a quest to be and do exactly what the scriptures said with no doubt or unbelief. Beloved, I pray for you to have this same reaction of such a great Salvation.

CHAPTER SIX

The Great Salvation

"To have faith and believe is not for ourselves but rather that God will do the right thing for us."

—John Gold

THUS FAR WE NOW UNDERSTAND HOW SIN came to be and the effects of our sinful nature from Adam and Eve. I have taken you through the physical, psychological and spiritual implications of what Christ did for us. Up until this point, we have known Jesus the man as a teacher or Rabbi, but an amazing transformation took place for all humanity. He arose out of that grave, transformed into our Savior and Messiah, and for forty days appeared to almost a thousand people in and around Jerusalem with a clear message of Salvation and walking in the Spirit. We moved from the law to grace. 4 For Christ is the end of the law for righteousness to everyone who believes. (Romans 10:4)

What are the qualifications for such a great Salvation? There are two located in Romans 10:9-10 9 that if you confess with your mouth the Lord Jesus and believe in your heart that God has raised

Him from the dead, you will be saved. 10 For with the heart one believes unto righteousness, and with the mouth confession is made unto Salvation.

These words of faith require confessing with your mouth and believing in your heart. I want to talk for a moment concerning two critical points: faith and belief. What is faith, and what does it mean to believe?

In Hebrew, the word faith is '*Emunah,*' meaning firm; something supported or secure. It is someone firm in their actions.

Faith in English is usually perceived as a knowing, while the proper Hebrew word, '*Emunah,*' is a firm action. To have faith in God is not knowing God, Jesus and the Holy Spirit, but rather having faith beyond any doubt they are true, and the Word of God and His promises are true beyond any doubt or fear.

Faith is our firm, secure belief that God, Jesus and the Holy Spirit are who they say they are and, in faith, we take laser-focused action concerning the Word and our relationship with Him. There is absolutely no doubt, fear or unbelief. It involves taking action to prove what the heart already knows. Faith without works is dead- James 2:14, 20, 26.

The Hebrew word for believe is '*Aman,*' which means stability and confidence; to be steady, firm and trustworthy. To believe is not only cognitive (the mental act of acquiring knowledge) but also personal, for we believe without doubting God's word of promise.

Faith and belief are crucial to God's plan of salvation, as can be seen in Romans 4 concerning Abraham. There was simply no way that anyone except Christ could ever be sufficiently righteous to meet God's standards and avoid His wrath. Having faith in God and believing in Him was not in itself something that could be a substitute for perfect righteousness, but God graciously determined to accept our faith and our believing as an equivalent for that righteousness nonetheless. So, in a sense, we received salvation and righteousness on credit, and the bill for that salvation and righteousness was paid by the death of Jesus on the cross.

Beloved, just because someone walked up the aisle of a church and repeated some words of a pastor does not mean they are saved. Salvation is not repeating something someone else says. It requires faith and believing. More salvations happen in homes, on the side of the road, in bars, etc., because people have simply come to the end of themselves and there is nothing left in them and no other place to turn. In those desperate hours is when many salvations occur as the lost turn to God and, trust me as one who knows, you will have faith and believe once you come to the end of yourself.

Many refuse to receive Jesus because they don't think they are clean enough, worthy enough or simply don't believe. Many feel what they have done to this point in life is too ugly to receive such a free gift. There is nothing you can do to come to a point where you are cleaned up enough. There will never be enough bars of soap, so to speak, because it is not you who can do anything, but rather it's what Christ did for you on the cross.

A blood sacrifice has always been a requirement for the atonement of sin, and only the sinless and perfect blood of Jesus can cleanse us and make us clean. We can't do it for ourselves. We must accept the free gift of His Salvation and righteousness through His blood. He is the only way. He died to save you, and it was His love that made Him choose to give His life for yours. Jesus will meet you today, right where you're at and, in the condition, you're in. You simply must believe, have faith and confess Him.

We need to take faith and believing much more seriously. Most of the non-believing world see many Christians as hypocrites and liars because most don't truly have the faith and believe. Our brothers and sisters in the Middle East have knelt and been beheaded because they believed and had faith unto death. In China and other places in the world, many are imprisoned, beaten, tortured because they will not relent their faith and belief. They stand firm in Jesus and the Word of God.

I see many believers living in condemnation, saying '*I am not a good Christian.*' or '*I am always doing this or that.*' Jesus said specifically in Romans 8:1 There is therefore now no condemnation to those who are in Christ Jesus, who do not walk according to the flesh, but according to the Spirit.

Friends, those believers who think, act and allow condemnation simply do not believe and have faith, and yet you see it in their words and actions. If condemnation tries to enter, you slam that door shut and say "*NO! I believe what Jesus said, period! Now get behind me devil.*" I call it, simply, the spirit of stupid. To be under condemnation when Jesus said there was none, in my opinion, is a spirit of antichrist because it is anti-Jesus. It is not faith and belief; it is fear, doubt, and unbelief. Jesus is pretty black and white. There is no grey area in Him or His Word. We need to celebrate our salvation, faith, and belief. Shout for joy that in Him we are not condemned, but righteous, mighty, the head and not the tail!

CHAPTER SEVEN

More than just Salvation

"The reality of loving God is loving him like he's a Superhero who actually saved you from stuff rather than a Santa Claus who merely gave you some stuff."

—Criss Jami

W HAT ELSE DO YOU RECEIVE upon salvation? This is exciting!

Access to God

At the moment of Salvation, we immediately have access to God and His Kingdom.

The Holy Spirit

Before Salvation, you had your flesh, soul (mind, will, and emotions,) and your human spirit. Upon Salvation, you receive the Holy Spirit inside you that connects to your human spirit. You now are a three-part being of flesh, soul, and Spirit connected to the Kingdom of Heaven. Ephesians 1:13, 1 Corinthians 2:12

Righteousness

You move from a state of unrighteous to righteous. The Hebrew word for '*righteous*' is 'Tsaddiq' (Tsad-deek) and means: blameless, justified, innocent, and in right standing with God. There is nothing you can do to become un-righteous before God ever again. Due to Jesus' sacrifice on the cross, you are forever seen by God as innocent and blameless, for we are complete in Him. Romans 3

Ambassadorship

You become an ambassador of the Kingdom of God. An ambassador of a country is a representative who is established in another country and represents in truth the rules, regulations, ideas, character, and values of the country he or she is an ambassador of. You are an ambassador of the Kingdom of Heaven, you are ruled by God, Jesus and the Holy Spirit, and the Word of God on this Earth. You are simply a visitor here on Earth, established as an ambassador of Christ Jesus. You carry with you credentials of diplomatic immunity of the Kingdom of God. You receive the seal of the Holy Spirit. 2 Corinthians 5:20, Ephesians 1:13-14

Eternal life

God the Father imputes His eternal life to us at Salvation. Simultaneously, God, the Holy Spirit enters us into union with Christ so that we share our Lord's eternal life. We have a double blessing of eternal life, (1 John 5:11-13.)

Eternal Security

Your Salvation is from the integrity of God, which was manifested at the cross by our Lord and Savior Jesus Christ. There is nothing

God the Father, God the Son, or God the Holy Spirit can do to cancel our Salvation after we believe in Jesus Christ, nor is there anything we can do, (John 10;29, Romans 8:38-39.)

Justification

Justification means a judicial act of vindication. We are born under condemnation, being spiritually dead. Justification is an official judicial act that occurs every time anyone believes in Christ. The justice of God acts on our behalf pronouncing us justified. This means having a relationship with God forever and having the perfect righteousness of God imputed to us. Justification is the judiciary act of God, whereby He recognizes we have His perfect righteousness, (Galatians 2:16, Titus 3:7 Romans 3:28.)

Sainthood

You are transformed into a saint and no longer can be called a sinner.

19 "Now, therefore, you are no longer strangers and foreigners, but fellow citizens with the saints and members of the household of God." Ephesians 2:19-22.

Entry to the Kingdom of God

We were formerly 'sons of disobedience,' and thus members of Satan's kingdom before salvation. However, we have been transferred into the Kingdom of God at the moment of Salvation, *"And [God] transferred us to the Kingdom of His beloved Son,"* (Ephesians 2:3, Colossians 1:13.)

Deliverance from the kingdom of Satan. At the moment you believe in Christ, you are delivered from the authority and power of the kingdom of darkness, *"For He delivered us from the domain of darkness."* Colossians 1:13.

Power and Authority

You are now infused with the full authority and power of Christ in you, and are above all demonic principalities, powers, and rulers of darkness.

Royalty

You are now royalty and part of a royal Kingdom family. Revelation 1:6.

Warriors for Christ

You now have the full armor of God upon you. Ephesians 6:10-18.

Spiritual Gifts

Spiritual gifts are designed to serve both God and other members of the body of Christ. All spiritual gifts are a matter of grace! No gift is given based on God's foreknown merit of the believer. The Holy Spirit sovereignty gives spiritual gifts to each believer at the point of salvation as He sees fit. 1 Corinthians 12.

CHAPTER EIGHT

How to gain Salvation

"Self-sufficiency is the enemy of salvation. If you are self-sufficient, you have no need of God. If you have no need of God, you do not seek Him. If you do not seek Him, you will not find Him."

—William Nicholson

THERE IS A WONDERFUL STORY in the Bible about the prodigal son I would like to use here.

Luke 15:11-32, The Parable of the Lost Son

11 Then He said, *"A certain man had two sons. 12 And the younger of them said to his father, 'Father, give me the portion of goods that falls to me.'"* So he divided to them his livelihood. 13 And not many days after, the younger son gathered all together, journeyed to a far country, and there wasted his possessions with prodigal living. 14 But when he had spent all, there arose a severe famine in that land, and he began to be in want. 15 Then he went and joined himself to a citizen of that country, and he sent him into his fields to feed swine.

16 And he would gladly have filled his stomach with the pods that the swine ate, and no one gave him anything.

17 But when he came to himself, he said, *'How many of my father's hired servants have bread enough and to spare, and I perish with hunger! 18 I will arise and go to my father, and will say to him, 'Father, I have sinned against heaven and before you, 19 and I am no longer worthy to be called your son. Make me like one of your hired servants.''*

20 And he arose and came to his father. But when he was still a great way off, his father saw him and had compassion, and ran and fell on his neck and kissed him. 21 And the son said to him, *'Father, I have sinned against heaven and in your sight, and am no longer worthy to be called your son.'*

22 But the father said to his servants, *'Bring out the best robe and put it on him, and put a ring on his hand and sandals on his feet. 23 And bring the fatted calf here and kill it, and let us eat and be merry; 24 for this my son was dead and is alive again; he was lost and is found.'* And they began to be merry.

25 Now his older son was in the field. And as he came and drew near to the house, he heard music and dancing. 26 So he called one of the servants and asked what these things meant. 27 And he said to him, *'Your brother has come, and because he has received him safe and sound, your father has killed the fatted calf.'*

28 But he was angry and would not go in. Therefore his father came out and pleaded with him. 29 So he answered and said to his father, *'Lo, these many years I have been serving you; I never transgressed your commandment at any time; and yet you never gave me a young goat, that I might make merry with my friends.'*

30 *'But as soon as this son of yours came, who has devoured your livelihood with harlots, you killed the fatted calf for him.''*

31 And he said to him, *"Son, you are always with me, and all that I have is yours. 32 It was right that we should make merry and be glad, for your brother was dead and is alive again, and was lost and is found."*

Beloved, we need to come to the end of ourselves. We are selfish and stubborn people. We don't like help and, in our pride, believe we can do it all ourselves. Sooner or later, you will come to a place of surrender. A place where we cannot take another step as the world we created begins to unravel. By the time we get to this place we have typically left a wake of destruction behind us and, like the prodigal son, we find ourselves in the pen with the swine. To gain Salvation, we need to come to the end of ourselves and admit we need help. Man and his wisdom have left us in turmoil and alone. When we come to ourselves, we are then ready to gain Salvation.

How you gain Salvation

9 That if you confess with your mouth the Lord Jesus and believe in your heart that God has raised Him from the dead, you will be saved. 10 For with the heart one believes unto righteousness, and with the mouth confession is made unto salvation. 11 For the Scripture says, *"Whoever believes on Him will not be put to shame." 12 For there is no distinction between Jew and Greek, for the same Lord over all is rich to all who call upon Him. 13 For 'whoever calls on the name of the Lord shall be saved.'"* (Romans 10:9-13)

Beloved if you have come to the end of yourself. If you will have faith and believe, if you cry out to the Lord confessing Jesus is who He said He is and believe in your heart of hearts that God raised Jesus from the dead, then congratulations, you are righteous, a new person, and are now saved. You are no longer a sinner but now a saint in His Kingdom. Now go share the good news!

CHAPTER NINE

Leading others to Jesus

"Jesus promised his disciples three things—that they would be completely fearless, absurdly happy, and in constant trouble."

—William Barclay

I BELIEVE THIS VERY THING. You cannot speak of something with any integrity (people can ramble on all the time without knowing what they're talking about) unless you have experienced it. Only one has ever walked in your shoes, and that's you. Only you know the exact place and time that you came to the end of yourself. Only you know the agony of your own torment and when you came to know that Jesus was your only hope, your Salvation. Now, in Christ, you can identify with love, acceptance and a feeling of belonging by personal experience of what you yourself went through when you gained Salvation. This is called your personal testimony, and it is the greatest experience you can share with someone else.

I did practical street research. When I saw someone with a Jesus shirt on, a person with the fish symbol on their vehicle or someone wearing jewelry or a tattoo that spoke of Jesus, I would confront them, posing as an unsaved person, and then would ask them to lead me to salvation. Ninety-five percent of the time I received a look from the person like a deer in headlights. They would stammer for the words or go into a speech that never led me to Salvation. They had no clue how to do the most basic truth, how to lead someone to Salvation, so I am going to teach you how to share Jesus with others so that you will be great at it.

I saw a person in the parking lot of our local grocery store. They were driving around, obviously frustrated and in a rush to find a parking space. You could see them yelling, waving their hands about, and then I spotted it: a Jesus fish symbol on the back of their vehicle. I waited for them to park and purposely put myself between them and the entrance of the grocery store. I said, *"hello, I am John, and I have a question for you."*

Of course, they looked at me impatiently. I continued and asked what that fish thing was on the back of their vehicle. A look that seemed to say, 'oops, I just got my hand caught in the cookie jar' appeared on their face, and their demeanor began changing from one of frustration to becoming childlike. They told me it was a symbol of someone who follows Christ. So, I said, *"oh, you're a Christian?"* They said, *"yes."* I stated, *"that's amazing, what perfect timing that I ran in to you. You see I am not saved, and I want to be saved. Can you lead me to Christ?"* The deer in the headlights look came upon them as they began to stammer and search for a response. The person wound up giving me a phone number to a friend of theirs and said I should call it.

Now what do you think the conversation was that they had within themselves after that encounter?

How you start your day matters.

1. Thank God for who He is; thank Him for his character and nature. Speak this out loud from a grateful and joyful heart.

Abba (Hebrew for father) I thank You for this day You have made. I thank You for Your grace, mercy, and love. I thank You that You are omniscient (knowing everything), omnipotent (having unlimited power to do anything) omnipresent (present everywhere all at once). I thank You that in You are all things and You have providence over all. I am humbled Abba that before You created anything, You thought of me first.

2. Ask the Holy Spirit to search the deep things of God on your behalf.

10 But God has revealed them to us through His Spirit. For the Spirit searches all things, yes, the deep things of God. 11 For what man knows the things of a man except the spirit of the man which is in him? Even so no one knows the things of God except the Spirit of God. 12 Now we have received, not the spirit of the world, but the Spirit who is from God, that we might know the things that have been freely given to us by God. (1 Corinthians 2:10-12)

3. Ask the Holy Spirit to order your steps for that day. Ask Him to place before you anyone who needs a touch of Him today.

(I am handing over my will to fulfill the will of the Father)

23 The steps of a good man are ordered by the Lord, And He delights in his way. (Psalm 37:23)

4. I ask the Holy Spirit for your daily bread. (Ask the Holy Spirit for a scripture for the day that you can meditate on.)

Faith in Christ brings things towards you. Faith brings people and situations to you, you do not have to go out and find people to minister to, the Lord will create a circumstance, and you will meet someone who needs a touch of God. I cannot count how many times I am just going about my day, and suddenly I am in a situation where the topic of Jesus is brought up. I have led many to Salvation, healing, given words of wisdom or knowledge and simply prayed for someone. These encounters happen on a weekly and sometimes a daily basis and it will for you, too.

In the situation of Salvation, you will meet someone and a conversation will begin. It can be a phone call, while you're shopping, getting gas or sitting in a restaurant. You will know within you by the Holy Spirit that yes, you are to lead this person to Salvation.

1. Listen to them.
2. Share your testimony of how you gained Salvation.
3. Show and explain Romans 10:9-13.
   a. You can open a bible app on your phone and have them see it and read it.
4. Briefly explain what it is to have faith and believe.
5. Ask them if they would like to join the royal family.
6. Be there to support them, but they must do this on their own as it is personal between them self and Jesus.

Congratulate them and exchange information so you can reach out and check on them and answer any questions they may have. It's that simple.

CHAPTER TEN

Testimonies

"The greatest single cause of atheism in the world today is Christians, who acknowledge Jesus with their lips, walk out the door, and deny Him by their lifestyle. That is what an unbelieving world simply finds unbelievable."

—Kevin Max

TESTIMONY #1

IN THE WINTER OF 1999 I WAS stationed at Fort Hood, TX after serving a twelve-month tour near the DMZ (Demilitarized Zone) in Korea for the U.S. Army. Unfortunately, in the winter of 1998, I was injured during a field exercise in Korea. I received a traumatic brain injury and spinal cord injury, and as a good soldier sucked it up, mission first, and ignored my injuries. I was on painkillers, muscle relaxers and drinking pretty heavily for the pain. Three months before I rotated to Fort Hood, I had learned my wife had been cheating on me the entire time I was gone.

A few hard months later in the spring of 2000 at Fort Hood, I was again in the field. With my squad in tow, we made a quick trip back to grab showers, change uniforms and feed my soldiers. I was dropped off first, and as I walked in, I noticed everything was gone. My step kids, most of the furniture, and my truck. On an end table next to the recliner was a note and my wife's wedding ring. Fear gripped me.

I told my soldiers to go ahead without me and inform the first sergeant I would not be returning to the field. An hour later my first sergeant showed up and brought me to company headquarters where we met the company commander and a chaplain. They were very supportive and wanted to be sure I was not going to do anything stupid. I told them I was good. The CO. gave me a four-day pass and told me to take it easy, and I returned to my house off post.

I was devastated, to say the least, as I sat in my recliner, staring at my medications and a bottle of Jack Daniels on the kitchen counter across the room. It felt like I came out of myself as I stood up, walked over, took every last pill from the bottles and swallowed them all, chasing it with the rest of the ½ a fifth of Jack Daniels. I vaguely recall falling to the living room floor a short time later.

'*Where am I?*' I thought to myself. I was so cold, could not move and surrounded amid a blackness I have never experienced. I felt I was in the middle of outer space. I felt I was floating like in a suspended state of animation. A small dot of white light came and grew bigger as it came to me; it formed, and suddenly Jesus was before me in radiant white. Loudly, He spoke. "*Stop blaming your lot in life on others! I will return you, and you can stay as you are or you can pick up your cross and follow Me!*"

Suddenly I came to and knew I was on the floor of the living room. Rigor mortis set in and it took me what seemed hours to open my eyes and begin to be able to move. It was learned later I had been dead for two days. I crawled to the shower and then crawled into bed and slept for fourteen hours. The doorbell rang and there stood my old roommate— *'the preacher'* as we called him in Korea—and Ed never missed a beat. He looked me up and down and simply said, "be at the church at seven p.m." Then he left.

Ed was always on me to attend his stupid little Podunk church. While it wasn't far—it was even inside our own neighborhood, Copperas Cove, just outside Fort Hood—I still struggled to find the motivation to actually get up and go.

At seven p.m., I walked inside the church and sat in the back. An apostle from Africa was speaking that night, and I rolled my eyes as I sat down with anger filling me. I could not understand why this anger was welling up inside me, but it did and it got worse. As I sat, suddenly it felt like something grabbed me, picked me up and was leading me to the front where this apostle guy was ministering. The closer I got to this man, the angrier I became until reaching the point where I wanted to murder this man of the cloth. What I didn't know or understand at the time was that it was an evil spirit within me.

I approached this man, and he laid his hands on my head. Based on witnesses there that night a battle ensued between something in me and this man. I went from anger to complete fear. I barely recall what ensued but remember asking him to save me. During this battle between a demon and this minister, I would come to myself only to be pushed back down as I stood there. I cried out, *'Jesus save me!'* And the next thing I remember I was lying on the floor. I awoke and felt as light as a feather, as if every care in the world was gone. I was at complete peace.

The next day at home I was listening to what Ed called 'worship music' when I hit my knees, and I was overwhelmed as I cried and travailed to Jesus. Everything came out of me; I told Him how sorry

I was for my past, and after about forty-five minutes of groaning and crying as I have never cried before, I felt a hand enter my chest and love I have never known came over me. I asked Jesus to save me. John Gold died that day, and I was made brand new.

The following Sunday, I was asked to give my testimony to the congregation of what transpired. After we had dinner together, Ed's little boy came up to me, tugged on my shirt sleeve and said, *"Hey mister, are you the man Jesus brought back from the dead?"* I was taken aback by the question and pondered it for a few moments. A big smile came across my face, and I responded, *"Yes. Yes, young man, I am the one."* The young boy hugged me and said, *"cool"* before running off to play with the other kids. A year later, I was called to ministry and never looked back. That was eighteen years ago. I love who Jesus created me to be and love the person I have become through Him.

We are the best of friends.

- J. Gold

TESTIMONY # 2

I accepted Christ at twelve years old, shortly after my father died. For a time, I was having recurring nightmares, and I didn't talk to anyone about them. Repeatedly, every night for weeks, I would have the same nightmares. There would be variations, and they might look slightly different, but they all were essentially the same thing. In every dream, I would be outside with a group of people. We might be in the woods, at an amusement park, near a body of water, at an outdoor concert; at some sort of outdoor gathering with a crowd of people. In the sky, there would always be objects appearing that were flashing, spinning or moving. They might look like ornaments, geometric shapes or even things I used that day at school like pencils, protractors, erasers or rulers. It could be during the day or night, but in each case, those objects symbolized to the crowd a sign that Jesus was returning right then. Some were ready. Most were not, and those that weren't were very afraid. You could feel the panic. I call these nightmares because I wasn't merely observing but was frantic too, because I was not ready and my Salvation was not sure. I had been taught to pray as a child at bedtime and before meals. My parents took me to Sunday school and church, but I wasn't ready, and I knew it.

One night I woke up very shaken, in a cold sweat and very startled. I just couldn't take any more of those nightmares. I slid off of my bed and onto my knees. I don't remember the words that I spoke, but I said them with my heart. The words aren't important, but in my own way I told the Lord that I wanted things to be right between He and me. I asked Him to forgive me of anything that I had ever done that hurt Him or anyone else. I asked him to accept me and allow me to go to Heaven when I died so that I could see my daddy again. This wasn't a canned prayer that someone else led me to say, just my own words pouring from my soul in the dark, on my knees with God listening to every word. That was the end of the nightmares. The following Sunday, when they gave an altar call, I marched down to the front of the sanctuary publicly showing what I had already done in secret that one morning, just Him and me.

- M. Moss

WORKS CITED

Edwards, William D., et al. On the Physical Death of Jesus Christ. American Medical Association, 1986.

Davis, C Truman. "The Passion of Christ from a Medical Point of View." Truth Archive, www.thecross-photo.com/Dr_C._Truman_Davis_Analyzes_the_Crucifixion.htm. New Wine Magazine, April 1982. Originally published in Arizona Medicine, March 1965, Arizona Medical Association.

Moss, A Melodie. Excerpt from a manuscript that is not yet titled.

God's Global Plan of Salvation by Philemon Yong, © 22 June 2018, pg. 18-26. Used by permission of Crossway, a publishing ministry of Good News Publishers, Wheaton, IL 60187, www.crossway.org."

SALVATION

LESSON ONE

JOHN GOLD

Identity Teaching Series

www.ingramcontent.com/pod-product-compliance
Lightning Source LLC
Chambersburg PA
CBHW031633040426
42452CB00007B/812